D1624827

1.4
.5 PT

Butterflies

by

Gail Saunders-Smith

Pebble Books

an imprint of Capstone Press

Pebble Books

Pebble Books are published by Capstone Press
818 North Willow Street, Mankato, Minnesota 56001
http://www.capstone-press.com
Copyright © 1998 by Capstone Press

Library of Congress Cataloging-in-Publication Data
Saunders-Smith, Gail.
  Butterflies/by Gail Saunders-Smith.
  p.cm.
  Includes bibliographical references (p. 23) and index.
  Summary: Illustrations and simple text describe the life
cycle of butterflies.
  ISBN 1-56065-485-6
  1. Butterflies--Life cycles--Juvenile literature. [1. Butterflies.]
  I. Title.

QL544.2.S29 1997
595.78′9--dc21
                          97-8315
                          CIP
                          AC

Editorial Credits
Lois Wallentine, editor; Timothy Halldin and James Franklin,
design; Michelle L. Norstad, photo research

Photo Credits
Michael P. Turco, cover, 1, 3, 4, 6, 8, 10, 12, 14, 16, 18, 20

Table of Contents

3

4

A butterfly lays
eggs on a plant.

6

The eggs grow.

8

The eggs become
caterpillars.

The caterpillars
eat the plants
and grow.

The caterpillars
turn into
chrysalises.

14

The chrysalises
turn into
butterflies.

The butterflies hatch.

Their wings dry.

The butterflies
fly away.

Words to Know

butterfly—a thin insect with large, often brightly colored wings

caterpillar—the worm-like stage of a butterfly's life

chrysalis—the middle stage of a butterfly's life; a chrysalis has a hard outer shell

egg—the beginning stage of a butterfly

hatch—to come out of an egg or chrysalis

Read More

Brust, Beth Wagner. *Butterflies.* San Diego, Calif.: Wildlife Education, Ltd., 1993.

Crewe, Sabrina. *The Butterfly.* Austin, Tex.: Raintree Steck-Vaughn, 1997.

Easterbrook, Michael. *The Concise Illustrated Book of Butterflies.* New York: Gallery Books, an imprint of W.H. Smith Publishers, Inc., 1991.

Heiligman, Deborah. *From Caterpillar to Butterfly.* New York: HarperCollins, 1996.

Internet Sites

Butterfly World
http:/www.introweb.com/butterfly

The Children's Butterfly Site
http://www.mesc.nbs.gov/butterfly.html

How to Make Butterfly Gardens
http://www.uky.edu/Agriculture/Entomology/ entfacts/misc/ef006.htm

North American Butterfly Association
http://www.naba.org/index.html

23

Note to Parents and Teachers

This book describes and illustrates the life cycle of the Atala butterfly, which is found in Illinois, Mississippi, and Florida. The clear photographs support the beginning reader in making and maintaining the meaning of the text. The noun and verb match the photograph on each page. The varied sentence types provide practice for the child to assume more control of the text. Children may need assistance in using the Table of Contents, Words to Know, Read More, Internet Sites, and Index/Word List sections of the book.

Index/Word List

Word Count: 41

24